BICYCLING
SANTA BARBARA

BICYCLING
SANTA BARBARA

BY
JOHN LEWIS

Drawings
by
Charles Newman

McNally & Loftin, Publishers
Santa Barbara

McNally & Loftin, Publishers
5390 Overpass Road
Santa Barbara, CA 93111

Copyright © 1983 by John Lewis

ISBN: 0-87461-050-8

Composition, Printing and Binding at
Kimberly Press, Inc.

TABLE OF CONTENTS

CENTRAL

WEST

EAST

SAN MARCOS PASS ROUTES

INTRODUCTION

Favored with excellent weather, a sea coast, a mountain range, and inland valleys within the reach of one-day rides, Santa Barbara is an exceptionally fine locale for the ambitious bicyclist. Within the urban area there are several bicycle paths and some streets with adequate bicycle lanes. The country, which in the direction of the mountains is surprisingly near, has interesting, lightly traveled roads, and in many places the busiest roads, such as Highway 101, are easy and safe for the cyclist.

All seasons of the year are good, so in Santa Barbara many citizens use bikes as their main mode of local transportation. These citizens are apt to be familiar with the recreational routes I describe in this manual, but newcomers and those new to bicycling should be interested. Even old-timers may find something in here that they have missed or would like to pass on in this form.

The routes, which vary in length from a few miles to 70 miles, are designed to be completed in one day, though on the longer routes there are campgrounds or motels that can be used for a stay over.

Most of the trips are described as loops, bringing the rider back to his/her starting point, where there is automobile parking in case the rider has used that shameful way of arriving. Obviously the loops can be joined at any point and taken in either direction. For the longer loops the author has tried to recommend the direction that will have the afternoon wind (from the west or northwest —along the coast) blowing on the cyclist's back.

Each route has a description in which mileages are given in parentheses, e.g. (4.7), a plan map, and an elevation map if the route is not flat or nearly flat. The difficulty of the route can be estimated by considering the distance and the amount of climbing that has to be done. As might be expected, the most spectacular rides, such as La Cumbre Peak, Casitas Pass, Refugio Pass, or Solvang, are the most difficult. Those with significant climbing are best done with a 10-speed bike or better, and they should all be undertaken with the usual precautions recommended in manuals on maintenance and safety.

1

CENTRAL

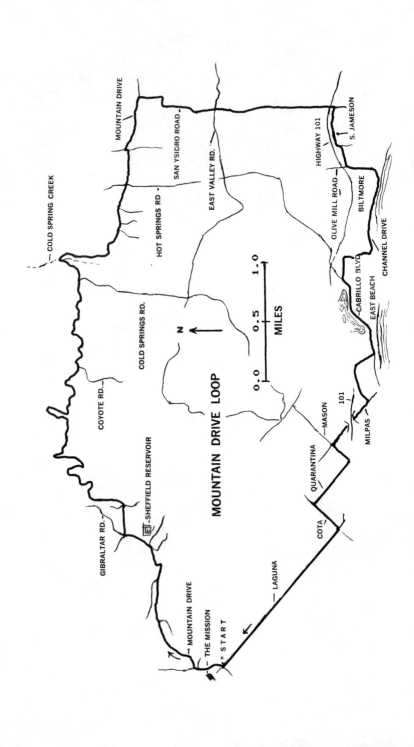

MOUNTAIN DRIVE LOOP

1

Mountain Drive Loop

This 16-mile ride takes you on the favorite road of many local cyclists (Mountain Drive), down through Montecito, and then along a fine beach before bringing you back to the Mission.

Start at the Mission ("Queen of the Missions"—dedicated in its present form in 1820). Head toward the mountains on Mission Canyon Road past the ruins of the Mission Aqueduct on the right and the Cota Sisters' Sycamores on the left. Take the second turn to the right on Mountain Drive (0.2) and stay on Mountain Drive for the next 7.5 miles. The climb starts immediately. At the Sheffield Water Reservoir turn to the left (1.4)—staying on Mountain Drive. The Santa Ynez Mountains, part of the only American Range that runs east-west, are straight ahead—La Cumbre Peak the highest with Cathedral Peak on its left. When you reach the

Mountain Drive.

Biltmore Hotel

junction with Las Canoas and Gibraltar Road (1.7), most of the climbing has been completed.

Mountain Drive now begins its winding, mostly level, course along the mountain slopes above East Valley. High above you can make out the cut made by Gibraltar Road, and out to sea the Channel Islands if the day is clear. Rincon Point juts far to the east. Along here the vegetation is chaparral.

On this blessed road cyclists and joggers usually outnumber automobiles.

The canyon through which Palm Park and Stearns Wharf come into view is Sycamore Canyon, site of the 1977 fire. After passing Cold Springs Road (5.6), a steep descent brings you to Cold Spring Creek—starting point of a popular hiking trail. The creek flows over the road year round and makes it slippery—careful!

Mostly down hill now until a short climb just before Hot Springs Road (7.1). The trip can be cut short by heading down into the valley on either Cold Springs Road or Hot Springs Road.

Leave Mountain Drive before it ends at the San Ysidro Ranch by turning right on San Ysidro Lane (8.2). If you wish to extend the ride toward Carpinteria, you can turn left on East Valley Road (Highway 192) (8.6) and follow the route described in the Carpinteria Loop, otherwise stay on San Ysidro until you have crossed Highway 101. Turn right immediately on to South Jameson, then left on Danielson, right on Virginia Road (10.0), and left on Olive Mill Road, which crosses the railroad tracks (10.3).

This road becomes Channel Drive as you pass between the Biltmore Hotel (classy resort hotel built in 1927) and Butterfly Beach. Just beyond the cemetery turn left on Cabrillo Boulevard or on to the bike path which parallels the Boulevard on its right. Andree Clark Bird Refuge is on the right and then East Beach on the left. Turn right on Ninos Drive (12.3), to pass the Childs Estate Zoo, then bear left on Punta Gorda to reach Milpas, turn right and cross back over the railroad tracks and under Highway 101.

At the northwest corner of Quinientos and Milpas, still alive, is the Sailors' Sycamore—a noble tree in a dismal setting. It was a landmark for ships around 1800.

At the next corner turn left on Mason, then right on Quarantina (dead end), then left on Cota (another dead end). Turn right on Laguna and climb back toward the Mission past the Santa Barbara Rose Garden, on the right, just before you reach your starting point (15.8).

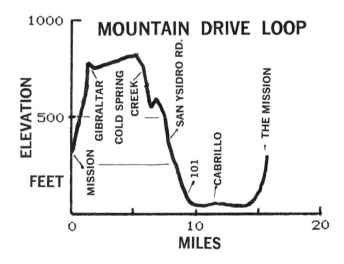

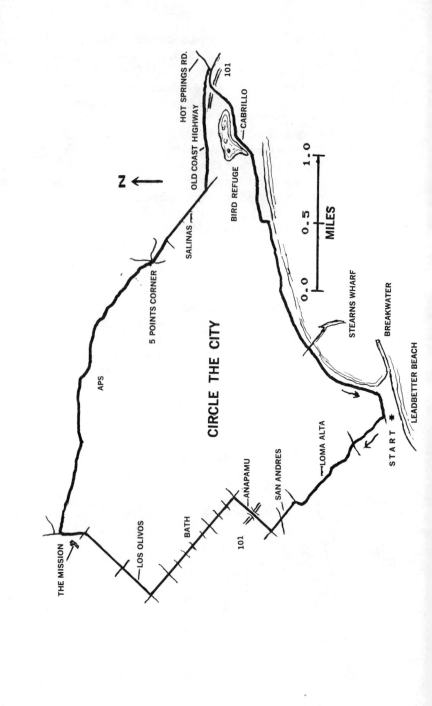

CIRCLE THE CITY

2

Circle the City

This ride is a relatively easy 11-mile loop around the main basin of Santa Barbara, providing good views of the city, first from the west, then from the east. It finishes with a ride along the popular, beach-side Cabrillo bicycle trail.

Start at Leadbetter Beach and take Loma Alta across Shoreline and past the City College Campus. Cross Cliff Drive and reach the high point of Loma Alta (0.5). Then descend and turn left on San Andres immediately at the bottom of the hill. Cross Carrillo and turn right at the next corner on Anapamu, using the pedestrian overpass to cross Highway 101 (1.4).

Turn left on Bath (1.7), a street with a generous new bike lane. The bike lane ends at Mission Street (2.5), but carry on past the Adult Education Center on the left.

Stearn's Wharf.

Then turn right on Los Olivos (2.6), pass the Mission on your left, and take the first right on to Alameda Padre Serra (APS) (3.5). This street climbs to a high point (3.9) where Lasuen Road branches off to the left. Just beyond Lasuen road is the last trolley car stop in Santa Barbara. Trolley cars ran here from 1876 until 1929. Pass the Jefferson campus of the Brooks Institute of Photography and descend to Five Points Corner (5.8). APS bears off to the left at the corner, but continue straight ahead on Salinas.

Before Salinas reaches Highway 101, turn left on Old Coast Highway (6.5), passing the Municipal Tennis Courts on the right and Montecito Country Club on the left. At Hot Springs Road (a dead end) (7.4) turn right making a U turn to double back on Coast Village Road. Get in the left lane immediately in order to turn left on Cabrillo Boulevard and pass under Highway 101 and the railroad tracks.

Fifty yards beyond the railroad tracks find the start of the Cabrillo Bikeway on the right. It will take you all the way back to Leadbetter Beach. The bikeway parallels Cabrillo Boulevard along the Andree Clark Bird Refuge and East Beach, but crosses the Boulevard at Milpas (8.7), then runs along the beach past Palm Park—Arts and Crafts exhibit and sale are held here every Sunday.

Stearns Wharf (9.8) with its shops and restaurants is a good side trip, as is the Yacht Harbor and Breakwater, which you pass just before the end of the loop at Leadbetter Beach (10.7).

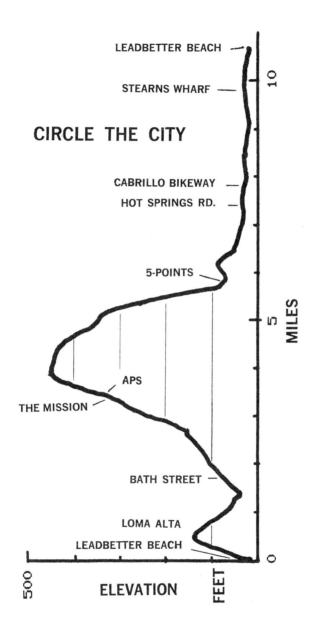

CIRCLE THE CITY

LEADBETTER BEACH —

STEARNS WHARF —

CABRILLO BIKEWAY —

HOT SPRINGS RD. —

5-POINTS —

APS

THE MISSION —

BATH STREET —

LOMA ALTA

LEADBETTER BEACH

MILES

10

5

0

ELEVATION   FEET

500

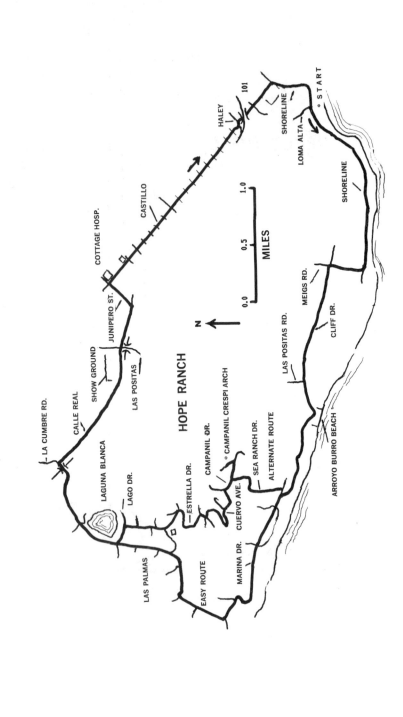

3
Hope Ranch

The main loop is an easy 12-mile ride that goes along the west shoreline of the city, through the central part of Hope Ranch, and then back through town on one of the better cycling streets of the city. A moderately difficult alternative route reaches a high point at the Campanil Crespi Arch overlooking the city from the west.

Start at the corner of Shoreline Drive and Loma Alta—Leadbetter Beach—and follow Shoreline Drive west on a climb to the top of Santa Barbara Point where Shoreline Park is located (0.4). You may ride the pathways through the park or stay on the drive. If you want to see the Santa Barbara Lighthouse, continue west on Lighthouse Place for about 75 yards beyond the corner where Shoreline turns right to become Meigs Road (1.5). The automatically operated lighthouse is in a small park.

High point of this first climb is 200 feet above sea level at the corner of Meigs and Cliff Drive (1.9). Turn left on Cliff Drive, which descends to Arroyo Burro Beach (3.1) at sea level before starting another climb that reaches an elevation of 150 feet above the shore at a vista point (3.9). The road turns right here and then left to become Marina Drive (4.0).

At this point you must choose to turn east (right) on Marina for the Alternate Route or west (left) for the easier route along Las Palmas Drive. The Alternate Route is only 0.4 of a mile longer but it climbs rapidly to 570 feet elevation. See the elevation map.

The easier Main Route continues west on Marina, becomes Roble Drive and then descends to a fork where it becomes Las Palmas Drive (5.4). Turn right on Las Palmas for a ride over gently rolling terrain. The roads through Hope Ranch have no shoulders and many curves, but the traffic is usually light.

After crossing Paloma Drive (6.2), Las Palmas becomes level

and straight. Lago Drive, the termination of the Alternate Route, joins Las Palmas from the right at 6.7 miles.

Alternate Route: If you choose the Alternate Route by turning right where Cliff Drive joins Marina, continue east on Marina for about 50 yards, then turn left on Sea Ranch Drive and head uphill for a tough half-mile climb. At the end of Sea Ranch (4.6) turn right on Campanil Drive, then left on Centinela Lane (4.7). The first building on the right is the Hope Reservoir of the City of Santa Barbara Water Department.

Laguna Blanca.

You can park your bike here and take a stairway to the left of the building or go 50 yards farther and take a rough dirt road up to the Campanil Crespi Monument (Campanil means free standing bell tower. Father Juan Crespi was chaplain to the 1769 Portola expedition). The tower has been vandalized but the view is unusual and possibly disorientating because of the unexpected prominence of otherwise obscure areas of the city.

Return to Campanil and follow it past Sea Ranch. Then turn left on Cuervo Avenue (5.2). Cuervo promptly reaches a dead end in a clump of bushes, but take a narrow path for about 10 yards through the bushes to reach a continuation of Cuervo. Where the street branches (5.4), take a hairpin turn to the left and down, still on Cuervo. Turn right on Estrella Drive (5.9) and follow this drive past Laguna Blanca School and several cross streets until it reaches a dead end at Lago Drive (6.9). Turn left on Lago and then right on Las Palmas (7.1) where the Alternate Route now joins the Main Route. Mileage given for the rest of the route will be that of the Alternate Route.

Las Palmas passes through the Hope Ranch Gate (7.7) and at a junction with Modoc Road becomes La Cumbre Road. Immediately after crossing Highway 101 turn right on Calle Real (8.1), a road that runs parallel to 101. After the Municipal Golf Course and the Earl Warren Showgrounds, cross Las Positas Road (9.3), then turn left on Junipero Street (9.6). Oak Park will be on your left. Turn right on Castillo Street (9.9) and follow it all the way to its end at Shoreline.

The first noteworthy buildings on this street are Cottage Hospital, the Sansum Clinic, and the Adult Education Center (at Padre Street). After crossing Mission (10.3), Castillo becomes one-way with a wide bike lane. The Hangman's Tree, where a murderer was hung in the 1890's, occupies part of the street just beyond Islay. Farther along there are **two** attractive Russian Orthodox churches, on opposite sides of the street.

The bicycle lane ends at Haley Street (11.8), but stay on Castillo anyway and pass under 101 (street is often wet and slippery here). Pershing Park is on the right just before you reach the end of Castillo (12.2). Turn right on Shoreline to arrive at the Loma Alta corner and Leadbetter Beach once again (12.7).

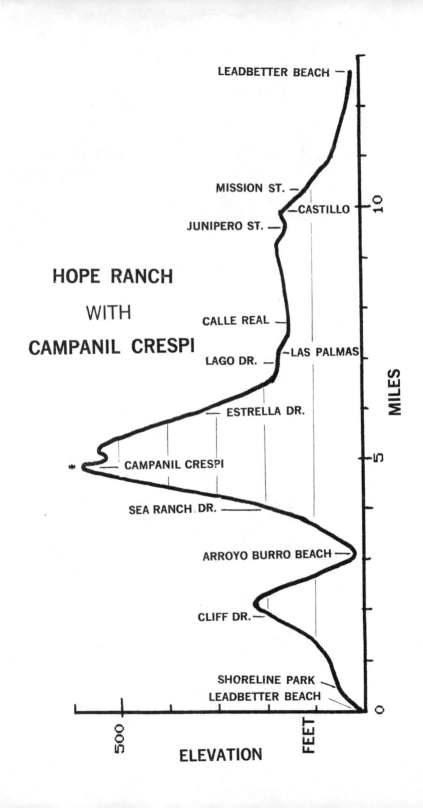

4

Sycamore -- Rattlesnake Trail

On this 8-mile ride you climb as high as East Casitas Pass, reach the starting point of the most popular hiking trail in the area (Rattlesnake Trail), and pass by or visit some of the best known local attractions: Botanic Garden, Natural History Museum, and the Mission. This is a good training ride for the longer, more difficult rides described in other chapters, with plenty of interest on its own.

Start at the Mission and take Mission Canyon Road toward the Mountains. Turn right on Alameda Padre Serra (APS) (0.1). Stay on APS until you get to Five Points Corner (2.4) where you encounter a STOP sign. Up to this point the route has been described in more detail under the City Circle Loop.

At the STOP sign turn left and take Sycamore Canyon Road through the canyon that was the site of the 1977 fire. Few scars of the fire are evident now. Chaparral regrows quickly and the home owners have rebuilt almost as fast. Here, as on other Santa Barbara roads that take you quickly into the foothills, you are suddenly out of the city and in the country. Five Points Corner, by the way, is the logical place to join this route from other parts of the city if you don't want to start at the Mission.

At the junction with Highway 192 (3.5) go straight ahead on Stanwood Drive. Best to strip down a little here because you are at the start of an uninterrupted 2-mile climb. Turn right on El Cielito Road (4.7)—still climbing. You can cut the ride short here by staying on Stanwood and taking Mountain Drive back to the Mission.

El Cielito crosses Mountain Drive (5.0), providing another escape route—still climbing. The upper part of Sycamore Canyon now opens up on the right with excellent views of two of the roads that are taken on other routes: Mountain Drive and Gibraltar Road.

17

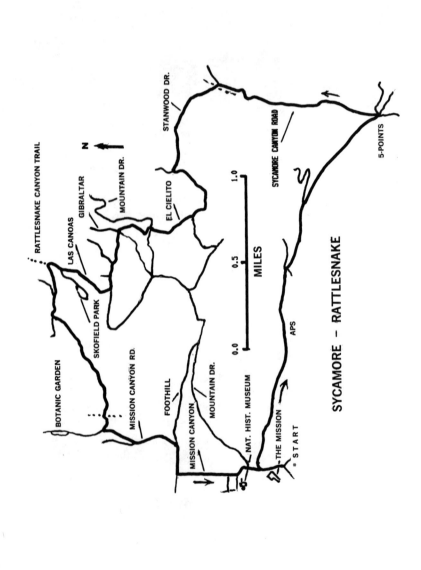

SYCAMORE – RATTLESNAKE

Rattlesnake Canyon Bridge —

Cross Gibraltar Road and pass the side road to Mount Calvary Monastery before turning right on Las Canoas Road (5.6). The high point of the ride (975 feet) is just ahead (5.7). Rattlesnake Canyon and Skofield Park are now below you on the left. A quick run downhill brings you to the bridge over Rattlesnake creek (6.0). The Rattlesnake trail-head is here; start from either side of the creek. Of course if your only objective in taking this ride was to reach the trail-head, you would have been better off by taking the loop in the reverse direction from the Mission. But you would have missed the climb—the beautiful climb.

There is a short climb away from Rattlesnake Creek, cresting at 6.2 miles, then it's downhill all the way back to the Mission.

Where Las Canoas ends at Mission Canyon Road (7.3), turn left. However, if you want to visit the Bontanic Garden, turn right for a short ride up to its entrance.

To reach the trail-head of another excellent hiking trail—Tunnel Trail—turn right on Tunnel Road (7.5) and ride a mile up Tunnel Road to its end.

When Foothill joins Mission Canyon (7.8), turn right and then at the STOP sign (7.9) turn left, again on Mission Canyon. At the street just beyond Las Encinas Road (8.2) the entrance to the Natural History Museum is on the right just 300 feet away.

Cross Mission Creek and you are back at your starting point, the Mission (8.6).

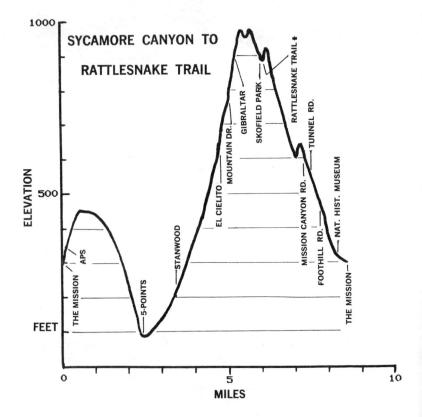

SYCAMORE CANYON TO
RATTLESNAKE TRAIL

ELEVATION

1000

500

FEET

THE MISSION
APS
5-POINTS
STANWOOD
EL CIELITO
MOUNTAIN DR.
GIBRALTAR
SKOFIELD PARK
RATTLESNAKE TRAIL *
TUNNEL RD.
MISSION CANYON RD.
FOOTHILL RD.
NAT. HIST. MUSEUM
THE MISSION

0   5   10

MILES

WEST

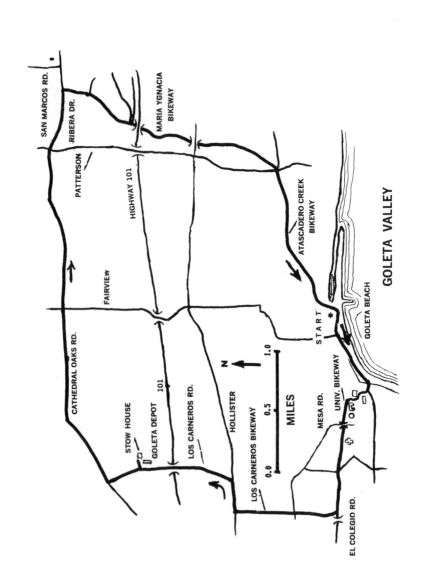

SAN MARCOS RD.

RIBERA DR.

MARIA YGNACIA BIKEWAY

PATTERSON

HIGHWAY 101

CATHEDRAL OAKS RD.

FAIRVIEW

STOW HOUSE

GOLETA DEPOT

101

LOS CARNEROS RD.

HOLLISTER

LOS CARNEROS BIKEWAY

ATASCADERO CREEK BIKEWAY

GOLETA BEACH

START

MESA RD.

UNIV. BIKEWAY

EL COLEGIO RD.

N

MILES

0.0   0.5   1.0

GOLETA VALLEY

5

Goleta Valley

The terrain of this ride is quiet compared to that of some of the more spectacular rides; but there are some charming woodland areas along the bike trails, auto traffic is absent to light, Goleta Beach (the starting point) is one of the most beautiful beaches in the area, the route is level, and it introduces the rider to several bike trails: Atascadero Creek Bikeway, Maria Ygnacia Bikeway, UCSB Bikeways, and Los Carneros Bikeway. Stow House—the Goleta Valley Historical Society Museum—and the nearby Goleta Depot are, when open, good stopping points.

Head west from Goleta Beach toward the University on the bike trail, take the left branch of the first fork (0.1); the right branch would take you past the airport to Fairview Avenue. Uphill then past a small but odiferous sewage treatment plant to the west border of the University where you cross Lagoon Road (0.5) and enter the campus bike trails. The campus map which is part of the Coal Oil Point route description may help here.

Turn right just beyond the motorcycle parking lot. Then the trail bends left with the Chemistry Building on your right. Just beyond the Chemistry Building (0.8) turn right on the trail through a large bike parking lot. Phelps Hall is now on your left. The trail turns left behind Phelps Hall and is easy to follow through the rest of the campus.

Cross Ocean Road at the west edge of the campus (1.5) and continue on the bike path which runs parallel to El Colegio Avenue. Just before this path dips down under Los Carneros Road (1.8), however, turn right on the Los Carneros Bikeway and follow it to its end at Hollister Avenue (2.7). Before turning right on Hollister, note the large Clenet auto plant on the far left corner of the intersection. There, I am told, artisans build vehicles for personal travel that are sold for $75,000 each—the other end of the spectrum from the thing you are riding on.

The Risk of Riding

Crouched as a fugitive
runs, without
the stability of a runner,
he spins angular legs
in circles as required by
wheels,

moves with a balance
that expires when he stops
spread eagled at the traffic sign
holding up a briefly
useless machine,

looks around, skeptical eyes
heedful of trucks, cars, mopeds,
motor cycles,
dull pedestrians, rash dogs,
all the shocks that
traffic may inflict,

rides on, skin chilled
by the breeze of motion,
muscles alive and straining,
attentive to the precious
moment, filled with the risk
of riding.

Turn left on Los Carneros Road (3.0) and cross Highway 101. The Goleta Depot (3.8), recently transplanted from its natural habitat at the railroad tracks and rebuilt, appears on your right and just beyond it the Stow House—dedicated as a Museum in 1967.

Goleta Depot

Los Carneros ends at Cathedral Oaks (4.1). Turn right. Why "Cathedral" Oaks? Religious camp meetings were once held under the high-arching branches of the oaks that grew here, particularly along San Antonio Creek. The road now is broad and level with no camp meetings but with adequate shoulders for cyclists.

Pass Fairview and Patterson Avenues and then, just beyond the Foothill School, turn right on Ribera Drive (7.5). By the way, this route. taken as described or in reverse, is a good way to get from the University or Isla Vista to the starting point of the San Marcos Pass Routes; for at this point, if you would continue another 0.2 mile on Cathedral Oaks, you would arrive at San Marcos Road.

Where Ribera Drive intersects with Pintura Drive (7.7), you have arrived at the start of the Maria Ygnacia Bikeway. It runs along the right side of Ribera Drive with the creek on its right. Cross University Drive (8.0) and continue on the trail. Just before the trail passes under Highway 101 there are two forks. Take the right-hand branch of each. The other branches are short spurs of the trail arriving from San Marcos Road.

At the next fork again take the right-hand branch (8.5) and cross the creek, then pass under Hollister Avenue (8.9). When this trail joins the Atascadero Creek Bikeway (9.6), turn right and follow it back to your starting point at Goleta Beach (11.2).

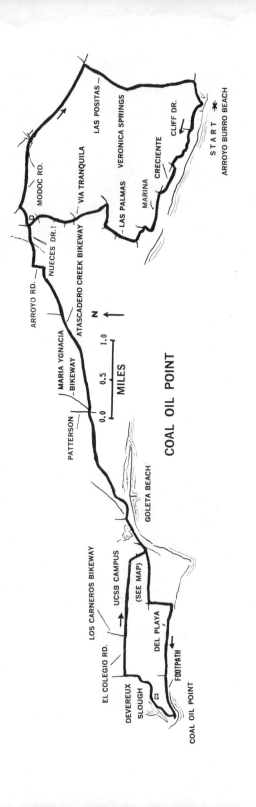

COAL OIL POINT

ARROYO BURRO BEACH

START

CLIFF DR.

CRECIENTE

MARINA

VERONICA SPRINGS

LAS POSITAS

LAS PALMAS

VIA TRANQUILA

MODOC RD.

ATASCADERO CREEK BIKEWAY

NUECES DR.

ARROYO RD.

MARIA YGNACIA BIKEWAY

PATTERSON

N

0.0   0.5   1.0
MILES

GOLETA BEACH

LOS CARNEROS BIKEWAY

UCSB CAMPUS

(SEE MAP)

EL COLEGIO RD.

DEVEREUX SLOUGH

DEL PLAYA

FOOTPATH

COAL OIL POINT

6
Coal Oil Point

This relatively level 23-mile route follows quiet roads in Hope Ranch and bicycle trails in Goleta and through the University to reach an isolated beach at Coal Oil Point. It starts at another fine beach—Arroyo Burro—and passes still another one—Goleta Beach —on the way.

From Arroyo Burro Beach head west on Cliff Drive for a climb that brings you to an elevation of 180 feet in 0.5 miles. Since this is the only significant climb of the route, no elevation map is given. Cliff Drive becomes Marina Drive (0.8) before you turn left on Creciente (0.9)—or simply continue on Marina if you miss the Creciente turnoff. Creciente returns to Marina (1.4) which then is renamed Roble Drive (2.0) after a couple of sharp turns. Turn right on Las Palmas (2.3), (on the left is the road to Hope Ranch's private beach), and continue through Hope Ranch, a subdivision for fine homes that was laid out by the Southern Pacific Railroad Company.

Turn left on Via Tranquila. At the crossing of Vieja Drive (3.9) Tranquila becomes Nogal Drive and passes Vieja Valley School. Just beyond the school parking lot, cross the bridge and turn left immediately on Nueces Drive (4.1). The route now is the Atascadero Creek Bikeway which goes all the way to the University (UCSB).

A sign on Nueces says "Not a Through Street," but carry on anyway; the bike trail crosses Atascadero Creek (4.3), on a bridge too narrow for cars. When Nueces reaches a dead end, turn left on Arroyo Road, cross the creek again, and then turn right on the trail. It follows the creek through the backyards of Goleta housing developments.

Just before Patterson Avenue, Maria Ygnacia Bikeway branches off inland to the right (6.7). Explore it on the Goleta

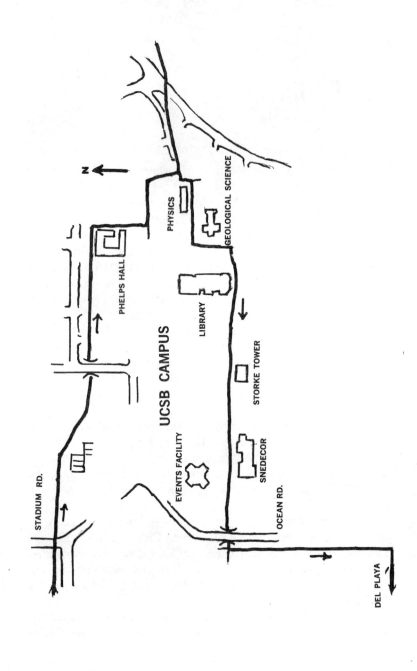

Valley Trail, but this time go straight ahead crossing Patterson and reaching the Goleta Beach entrance road (8.2). Turn left on the entrance road and follow the arrows for a right turn that keeps you on the trail. At a trail branch, bear left, make a brief climb, cross Lagoon Road and enter the University Campus (8.8).

The Campus (merely a Marine Officer Training Camp during WWII, by the way) has a network of bicycle trails. You'll make it through all right if you check the campus map and keep heading in the general direction west. More specifically, at the first opportunity turn left and then right on a broad brick-colored walk (not labeled as a bikeway). Physics will be on your right and Geological Sciences on your left. Turn left on the bike trail and then right. The library will now be ahead on the right and the Storke Bell Tower straight ahead. Stay to the right of the bell tower and pass between Snedecor Hall and the Events Facility. Then go under Ocean Road and turn left immediately on the bike path that parallels Ocean Road heading toward the Ocean.

At its end turn right on Del Playa Drive (10.1), and stay on Del Playa, which runs parallel to the shoreline, until its end (10.9).

Go west for 0.7 miles on a rough dirt footpath along the shoreline cliffs. A cluster of abandoned buildings stands on Coal Oil Point (11.4), which was dedicated as a natural reserve in 1973. Follow a dirt road past the buildings to reach a chain link fence (11.5). You'll have to park your bike here if you want to walk through the gate to a spacious and strikingly beautiful beach that has been kept relatively inaccessible to those who depend on cars. Enjoy it!

Coal Oil Point

Start the return by taking the dirt road away from the beach, back past the buildings, and through a fence where the road becomes hard surfaced. Devereux School is on the right and Devereux Slough (11.9), an excellent place for bird watching, on the left. Pass a guard house that restricts automobile traffic into the area and turn right on El Colegio Road. Ride on the concrete walk on the inland side of the Road; it is the beginning of the bike trail that will lead through the campus again and back to the Atascadero Creek Bikeway.

When El Colegio Road turns to the right (13.5), cross Stadium Road and follow the trail through the playing fields. If the University is in session, this is the busiest biking area in town. Turn right sharply beyond Phelps Hall, and then when the trail reaches a dead end, turn left. Turn left again when the trail joins a vehicular road and head east, leaving the campus (14.5) by the same trail on which you entered it.

Retrace your course on the trail until you reach Nogal Drive (19.1). Now go straight ahead on the trail to its end at Modoc Road (19.4). Turn right on Modoc Road and then right on Las Positas Road (21.5). The mileage markers you see on the shoulders along here are for the Santa Barbara Marathon, by the way. Veronica Springs Road (22.1), which you pass on the right, once led to a medicinal spring that was popular (along with Hot Springs in Montecito and Burton Mound) when Santa Barbara was a health spa in the 19th century.

Turn right on Cliff Drive when Las Positas reaches its end to arrive at Arroyo Burro Park once again (23.3).

EAST

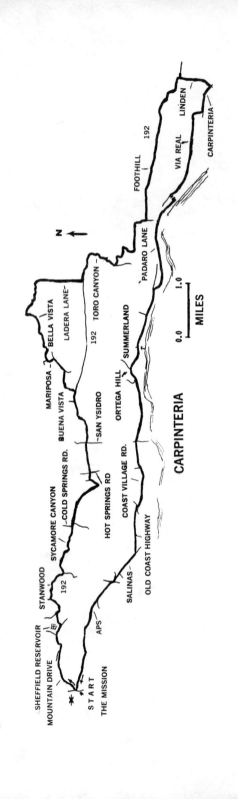

7

Carpinteria -- With Bella Vista

Depending on whether you take the Bella Vista alternative or not this is a moderately difficult or difficult 30-mile loop through Montecito, the foothills above Summerland, Carpinteria, Summerland, and the east side of Santa Barbara.

Head toward the mountains from the Mission and take the second turn to the right on Mountain Drive (0.2). Until reaching the Sheffield Reservoir, the route is the same as the Mountain Drive Drive Loop. At the Sheffield Reservoir corner stay on Highway 192 (Mission Ridge Road at this point) (1.4), which you will follow for the next 5.6 miles—until the turnoff on Buena Vista for the Bella Vista alternative.

On Highway 192 Mission Ridge leads into Stanwood Drive for a downhill ride to the junction with Sycamore Canyon Road. Turn left on Sycamore Canyon (3.1) and climb, then up-and-down. Turn left on East Valley Road (5.0) and pass through a Montecito shopping district at the corner of San Ysidro and East Valley Road (5.9). Montecito, by the way, was first settled by Americans in 1855. The trip can be cut short here by turning right on San Ysidro; ride toward the ocean and follow the route described in the Mountain Drive Loop.

At Buena Vista Road (7.0) turn left for the Bella Vista alternative—a ride high above the valley that rivals Mountain Drive in scenic beauty. If the rider prefers to skip this climb, however, he can stay on Highway 192. To reach Bella Vista Drive, take Buena Vista, then straight ahead on Tollis, and left on Lilac (7.5). The road is slightly down hill just before you turn left on Mariposa (7.8) for the **steepest** short climb (0.2 miles) of all the routes described in this manual.

If you make it, turn right on Bella Vista for a rolling two mile ride. Starting point of the Romero Canyon hiking trail is found at a little over a mile along this road. At a right turn the road becomes Ladera Lane (10.2) which descends in a straight line to join East Valley Road (Highway 192) again (11.1).

Continue on 192 past the Toro Canyon Park turnoff (11.7), left on Foothill, right on Nidever Road, and then left on Foothill again, but always on Highway 192 until you reach Linden Avenue (16.6). Head toward the ocean and downtown Carpinteria (17.3) on Linden. Carpinteria, the carpenter's workshop—named because it was here in the 18th century that Spanish explorers found the Indians building plank canoes—has a fine State Beach Park with a camping area for bikers and hikers, and hot showers, all for 50 cents a night.

Carpinteria Beach

For the return trip go west on Carpinteria Avenue and right on 7th Street to cross Highway 101 (17.9), then immediately left on Via Real. Turn left on Padero Lane (19.6), passing back under 101, and continue on Padero Lane until it crosses over 101 (21.6) and joins Via Real again. Turn left on Via Real to reach Summerland (22.8). Summerland was created when the old Ortega Ranch on the eastern slope of Ortega Hill was cut up into tiny lots, 25 by 60 feet, and sold to members of a spiritualist society for $25.00 each.

Climb over Ortega hill (23.3) and take North Jameson Lane, parallel to 101. Pass through the shopping area on Coast Village Road. When Coast Village Road is about to pass down under 101, turn right on Hot Springs Road and then immediately left on Old Coast Highway which runs below the Montecito Country Club. Turn right on Salinas Street (26.9). At Five Points Corner (27.6) continue straight ahead on Alameda Padre Serra (APS). It reaches a dead-end at Mission Canyon Road (29.9) where you turn left to complete the loop at the Mission (30.0).

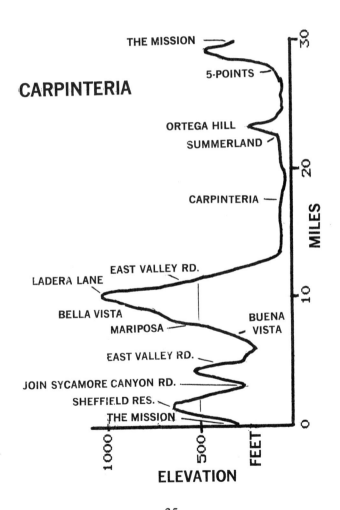

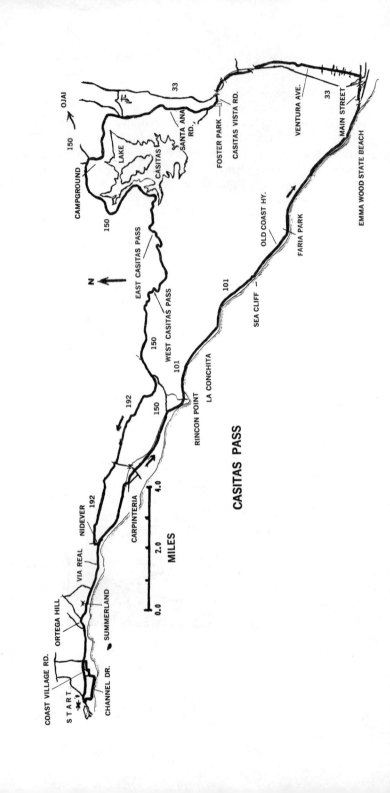

CASITAS PASS

8

Casitas Pass

This is a 62-mile loop into Ventura County, along the ocean and through the mountains, with a climb that reaches a high point of 1100 feet at East Casitas Pass.

Start at the east end of the Cabrillo Bikeway—the Andree Clark Bird Refuge. (With a start at Leadbetter Beach, this same route is the "Metric Century" of the Santa Barbara Bicycle Club's annual Century Rides.) Cross Cabrillo Boulevard and take Channel Drive past Butterfly Beach and the Biltmore Hotel (1.0) at which point Channel Drive becomes Olive Mill Road.

After crossing the RR tracks but before crossing Highway 101, turn right on Danielson, then right on South Jameson Lane, a street that runs parallel to 101. Turn left on Eucalyptus Lane, which is renamed San Ysidro Road as it crosses 101 (2.0). Turn right immediately on North Jameson Lane. From here until Ventura the route is the same as the Caltrans Bicentennial Bike Route. When Jameson forks, bear right and take Ortega Hill Road (3.2) over Ortega Hill and into Summerland (3.9).

Lille Avenue in Summerland becomes Via Real which reaches a dead end in Carpinteria (8.5). Turn right on Santa Ynez and cross 101, then left immediately on Carpinteria Avenue for a ride through town. The State Beach and Campground may be reached by turning right on Palm Avenue.

Continue on Carpinteria Avenue, and when it becomes Highway 150 (11.5), turn right and join Highway 101 going south. The wide shoulder of this noisy and scenic highway is the route for the next 5 miles.

At the Sea Cliff Exit (16.5) leave 101 and take the Old Coast Highway. Hobson Park is on the right and then Rincon Parkway begins. This parkway provides parking spaces, over the next 5 miles, for 322 Recreational Vehicles, in batches, interrupted by permanent dwellings and a beach. Some people use the RV's as their regular homes, obeying the two-week parking limit by moving from one campground to another. The road along here is wide, smooth, and lightly used—an excellent bikeway.

Faria County Park—a campground—comes up at 19 miles and then, about a mile farther along, an easily accessible beach.

At the Emma Wood State Beach entrance road (22.9) bear left taking the freeway entrance road instead, but don't enter the freeway. Rather, turn right on the bike trail (23.4) which begins just before the entrance road joins the freeway. This bike trail runs between the freeway and the railroad and above the State Beach for a little over a mile before it passes under 101 (24.6) and turns to the right to run parallel with Main Street, Ventura. After crossing the Ventura river (25.2), the bike trail turns to the right, but continue straight ahead on Main Street under Freeway 33 and then turn left on Ventura Avenue (25.6) heading north.

Even the best bicycle routes have bad stretches; for this route Ventura Avenue is it. Fortunately it clears up after about 3.5 miles. The road passes back and forth beneath Highway 33. Then before it joins 33, turn left and pass back under the freeway a final time, this time on Casitas Vista Road (31.0) headed for Foster Park.

The route now runs up the Ventura River Valley passing Foster Park (camping facilities), climbing slightly, and then turning to the right on Santa Ana Road (31.7). At Burnham Road (35.0) there is a grocery store which may interest you by now, but there is also a grocery store farther along at the Lake Casitas campground.

The climb is steady after Burnham Road until Wadleigh Arm of Lake Casitas comes into view (35.7), and the road levels out to follow the shore of the lake—water reservoir for the county, a popular fishing lake, and site for the rowing and canoeing events of the 1984 Olympics.

Recreational use of the lake centers around the campground (37.4), reached just before Santa Ana Road ends by joining Highway 150 (37.6). For a trip to Ojai—5 miles away—turn right on 150, but for our route over the Casitas passes, turn left and head west.

As the road runs along the irregular north shore of the lake for the next 4½ miles, it makes three climbs, descending back once again to the level of the lake after each one. Then it turns away

Wadleigh Arm - Lake Casitas

from the lake (42.1) and begins a steady climb up to East Casitas Pass (43.6)—elevation 1143. From here you will have a fine view of the lake and the Topatopa Mountains—snow-covered from a November storm the last time I was on the pass.

Coast downhill for 2 miles through the avocado groves that have replaced the chaparral in these hills before starting the climb to West Casitas Pass (46.3)—elevation 969. Just beyond the pass a view opens to the coast and the ocean before you dive down into the groves and the forest once again.

At the Santa Barbara County line (48.9), 150 heads south along Rincon Creek. Leave it by taking Highway 192 (49.6) for a brief climb away from the creek and into a relatively flat land of fruit orchards along the lower foothills. Stay on 192, crossing Linden Avenue (53.2)—the road to downtown Carpinteria. Then leave 192 finally at the polo grounds by turning left on Nidever (56.0). Turn right on Via Real (56.2), pass through Summerland and climb Ortega Hill once again (59.1)—it can't be avoided!

North Jameson becomes Coast Village Road (61.0) as you pass the Monticito Inn—once a famous Hollywood retreat (the song "There's a Small Hotel" was written about it), but now handicapped as a resort hotel by its nearness to noisy 101—and enter a Montecito shopping district. As the road heads down to go under 101 (61.7), get in the left lane and pass under 101 and the RR tracks. The bird refuge and the end of the trip are immediately before you (62.0).

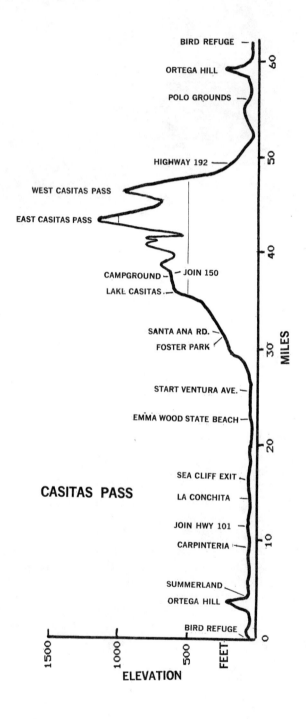

CASITAS PASS

BIRD REFUGE
ORTEGA HILL
POLO GROUNDS
HIGHWAY 192
WEST CASITAS PASS
EAST CASITAS PASS
CAMPGROUND
JOIN 150
LAKE CASITAS
SANTA ANA RD.
FOSTER PARK
START VENTURA AVE.
EMMA WOOD STATE BEACH
SEA CLIFF EXIT
LA CONCHITA
JOIN HWY 101
CARPINTERIA
SUMMERLAND
ORTEGA HILL
BIRD REFUGE

MILES

ELEVATION

1500   1000   500   FEET

SAN MARCOS PASS ROUTES

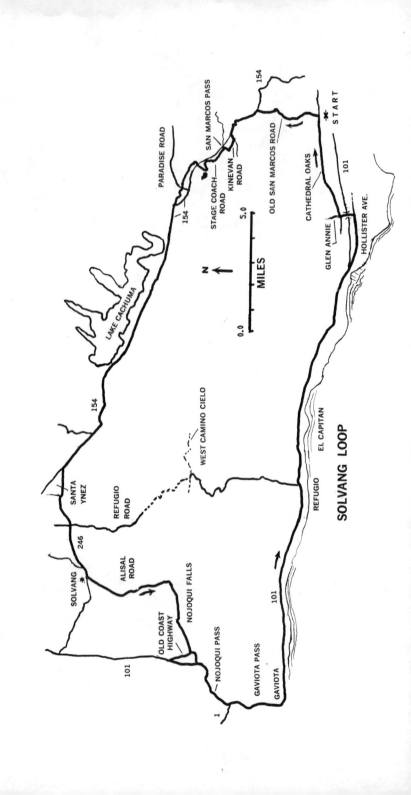

SOLVANG LOOP

9

Solvang Loop

This is a 70-mile loop offering magnificent scenery and a ride over two of the passes that have long provided access to the Santa Ynez valley from the Santa Barbara coast.

Start at the corner of Cathedral Oaks Road and Old San Marcos Road, and follow Old San Marcos Road for the first 3.5 miles—until it joins Highway 154. This route, which was once the Santa Ynez Toll Road, used by stagecoaches until 1901, is flat for the first 200 yards, until it passes a 300-year-old California Laurel in the middle of the street and crosses the Maria Ygnacia Creek. Then it begins a steady climb that will bring you to a 2200-foot elevation at San Marcos Pass.

After about 1.5 miles one has views of the Goleta Valley, the University, and the Channel Islands, and a little farther and on the other side of the road, views of the Maria Ygnacio Valley. Just beyond the Trout Club turnoff the road forks (3.5). Both branches meet 154 (3.6), the right branch crossing 154, to become Painted Cave Road. Take the left branch, join 154. and continue on it until West Camino Cielo (5.1). Turn left on West Camino Cielo and then after a couple hundred yards and the road has crossed San Jose creek, turn right on Kinevan Road. (The stagecoach tolls used to be collected at Kinevan's ranch.)

Kinevan Road rejoins 154 just before the high point of the pass (6.4), but you don't have to go back onto 154 here unless you want to cross it and go to the Cielo store and restaurant—about 50 yards up East Camino Cielo. Bear left and continue on Stage-coach Road for great views of the Santa Ynez Valley and the San Rafael Mountains and for a fast ride down past, or for a lunch at, the Cold Spring Tavern—once a stagecoach stop (8.3).

Stagecoach Road crosses Paradise Road (10.2) and continues another 1.5 miles before it rejoins 154 for an up-and-down course along Lake Cachuma (created by damming the Santa Ynez River in 1956). Pass the Lake Cachuma Campgrounds (17.3), cross the dry bed of the Santa Ynez River (21.5), and turn left on Highway 246 (23.7) to reach the town of Santa Ynez. A bicycle path parallels the road on the right, but the shoulders on the road are good along here.

Cold Spring Tavern

Beyond Santa Ynez you will pass the Indian Reservation Campground on the left (hot showers), and then cross Refugio Road (26.2). The route up to Refugio pass, past the President's Ranch, and down to Highway 101 is described in another section as the Refugio Pass Route.

Continue on to Solvang (28.7), a busy resort town, settled by Danes from the midwest in 1910, with many fine restaurants. Turn left on Alisal Road, which takes you across the Santa Ynez River again, past the Alisal Ranch resort complex, and along a lightly-traveled, tree-shaded, sunlight-dappled road to Nojoqui Falls County Park (35.3). Turn either right or left on Old Coast Highway and join Highway 101 for the climb over Nojoqui Pass. Then ride down through Gaviota Pass and to the Gaviota Rest Stop (42.6), reached before the Gaviota Beach Campgrounds (hot showers and a bikers' and hikers' section at 50 cents a night), and Gaviota itself (44.0) —a town consisting of a store and a restaurant.

The next 20 miles on the broad shoulder of Highway 101 is an up-and-down ride. If you're in luck, the afternoon winds will blow you rapidly toward Santa Barbara. To break the monotony of this leg, turn off at Refugio Beach and ride for 3.3 miles on the bike trail between Refugio and El Capitan State Beach. It is found on the left just after the Refugio Beach entrance road passes under the railroad tracks.

Leave 101 on Hollister Avenue (62.3). It was offshore near here in February, 1942 that a Japanese submarine surfaced and lobbed 25 five-inch shells ashore without doing much damage except to real estate prices which dropped sharply.

Turn left on Glen Annie Road (The road and Glen Annie Canyon were named after Col. Hollister's wife, Annie), then right on Cathedral Oaks Road and back to the starting point at San Marcos Road (70).

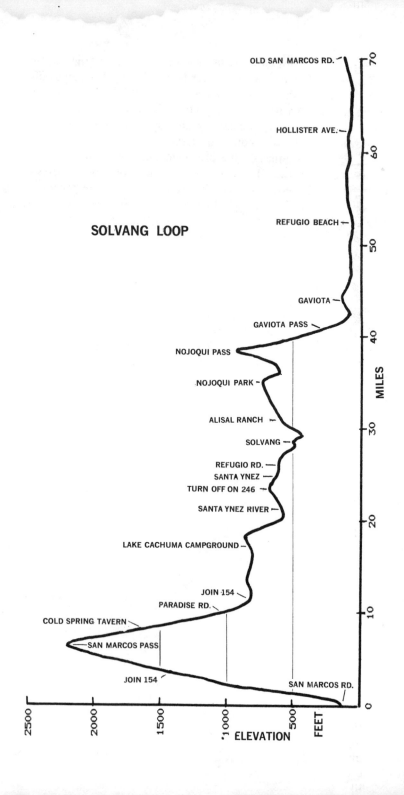

SOLVANG LOOP

10

Refugio Pass

You might think that the main reason for taking this route would be to bike past the President's ranch. It has that, but the route is a fine one without it. Because 3.4 miles on the north side of the pass are unpaved, that section is unpopular with cars, and you will have a beautifully quiet mountain road almost to yourself.

The road on the ocean side of the pass is also beautiful but a little busier. I suppose it might be quite busy when the President is in residence, but I haven't ridden it then.

Though not as long as the Solvang Loop, this route is made tougher by climbs over two, rather than one, 2200-foot passes. You miss the resort town of Solvang, but Santa Ynez has at least one good, and unpretentious, restaurant (Longhorn Coffee Shop).

For the first 26 miles follow the route described in the Solvang Loop, and use the Solvang plan map for the entire route. It shows Refugio Pass Road. Use the separate contour map for the Refugio Pass route.

Just west of Santa Ynez turn left on Refugio Road (26.2) and coast down hill to cross the Santa Ynez river on a narrow bridge (27.7). Once you are on Refugio Road, you will have no problem in route-finding—it's the only road. For 2.7 miles it runs along Quiota Creek, crossing back and forth and climbing gradually. Then the pavement ends, the road breaks away from the creek and begins a harder climb.

A sign says the road is "Impassable in Wet Weather." It may be after a long wet season, but the sign is meant for cars. I have ridden it 5 days after a heavy rain with no trouble. Hard packed dirt provides a surface you can bike on, though a washboard of stone eroding through the surface at the upper end of this 3.4 mile stretch of unpaved road might be hard on skinny, high-pressure tires (my own are 1¼ inch).

"The Gate" Refugio Road

West Camino Cielo, which goes along the crest of the range from San Marcos Pass, joins Refugio Road at the top of the pass (33.8). If you think you might like to take that road across from San Marcos some day, forget it. You can ride a bike on it for about 4 miles west of 154, then it becomes unmaintained gravel for the next 20 miles.

Though open only the first part of the week, a U.S. Forest Service station about 300 yards west of the pass has water available for the thirsty traveler at any time.

The side road to the President's ranch (3333 Refugio Road) (34.3), the first ranch on the way down, is unmistakable—gate with many locks, guard house, and slightly menacing TV monitors.

Below it the descent is uninterrupted and steep for about 5 miles. If you want to go fast, watch out for the two cattle gates. They could throw you; you can't ride over them.

As the road levels out, you pass through orchard country, cross the creek several times, and join Highway 101 (41.3) at the Refugio Beach Campground—another campground with a bikers' and hikers' section at 50 cents per night.

If you want to take the bike trail from Refugio Beach to El Capitan Beach, you can enter it by turning to the right off of Refugio Road just before the northbound entrance road of Highway 101. Turn left immediately after passing under the railroad tracks. The trail runs along the shore past a couple of nice beaches before joining the El Capitan Beach Campground Roads.

The route from Refugio Beach back to the corner of Cathedral Oaks Road and San Marcos Road (58.4) is the same as it is for the Solvang loop.

Refugio Pass

At the start
the profile of the mountains
conceals by its sharpness
the breadth of the range

that must be penetrated
on a narrow road
climbing and turning to
expose fresh canyons and
redundant hills

until the top of the pass,
long expected, comes as only a
commonplace stretch of road
no longer rising,

but farther on toward the
shore we see miles
of descending slope eroding
slowly under indifferent trees

that are fed by
crumbling stone and
meandering streams uncertain
in their provision.

Faster than the stream
a vacant road follows
a surveyor's course down
to its intersection

with the home bound highway
too vague at this distance to
mar the scene.

49

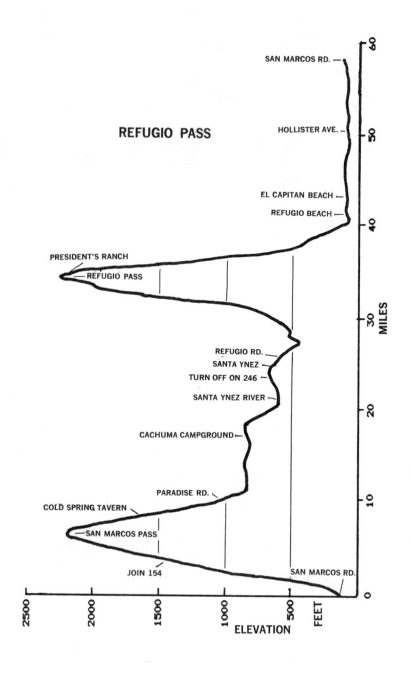

REFUGIO PASS

11

Painted Cave

This diffiuclt 15-mile ride takes you to an archeological land-
mark—the rock paintings of Painted Cave—then on and up to
East Camino Cielo at an elevation 500 feet higher than San Marcos
Pass before it descends to the Cielo Store and the pass.

As with the Solvang Loop, start at the corner of Cathedral
Oaks and San Marcos Road and follow the same route—the old
stagecoach route—until it joins Highway 154 at an elevation of
1410 feet (3.6). Where Old San Marcos Road forks at the covered,
concrete watering trough (3.5), take the right fork, which continues
across 154 as Painted Cave Road.

As alternatives you may choose to reach Painted Cave Road
by taking Highway 154 from the start, or by joining 154 part of
the way up after starting on San Antonio Creek Road—a continuation of Turnpike Road through Tuckers Grove (see the La
Cumbre Peak map). But most riders, including the author, avoid
154 whenever they can. San Marcos Road is quieter, more scenic.

Painted Cave Road itself is 3.3 miles long and a continuously
steep climb for its first 2.5 miles. Shortly after you are on it you
are looking down on 154, on the Old San Marcos Pass Road, and
at a greater distance, the Goleta Valley, the ocean, and the Channel
Islands. As the road turns toward the mountains, a colony of cliff-
top and cliff-side homes stands above you as a challenge. The route
ascends past them.

Before that, however, you reach Painted Cave (5.7). The road
is tree-shaded along here with a tributary of Maria Ygnacio Creek
below on the right (Chumash pictographs such as those found in
the cave are always found near permanent water). The cliff on the
left contains the north-facing cave with its entrance about 20 feet
higher than the road. There is no roadside sign indicating the site,
but the iron grill that covers the cave mouth can be seen from the
road.

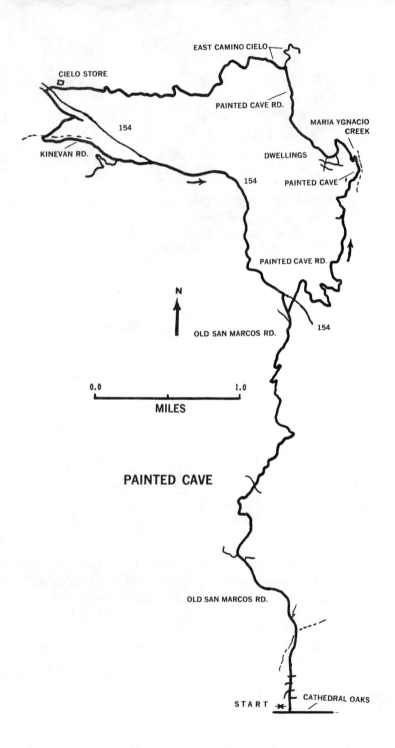

EAST CAMINO CIELO

CIELO STORE

154

PAINTED CAVE RD.

MARIA YGNACIO
CREEK

KINEVAN RD.

154

DWELLINGS

PAINTED CAVE

PAINTED CAVE RD.

N

154

OLD SAN MARCOS RD.

0.0   1.0

MILES

PAINTED CAVE

OLD SAN MARCOS RD.

START

CATHEDRAL OAKS

These abstract ceiling and wall paintings are believed to have been done by Chumash artist-shamans who were members of the *'antap* religious cult. The paintings may date back as far as 1000 years, but some evidence places their origin in the sixteenth or seventeenth centuries.

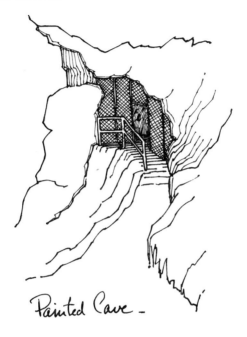

Painted Cave -

Beyond the cave the road continues to climb through oak savanah until it reaches a private road to the colony at 2620 feet (6.1). It climbs again before joining East Camino Cielo at 2780 feet, the high point of this ride (6.9).

Turn left on Camino Cielo and descend to San Marcos Pass and Highway 154 (9.0). Just before reaching 154 the Cielo Store is on the right. It has a new bar and an old restaurant where you can eat large, made-to-order sandwiches while seated on folding chairs at long tables covered with checkered oil cloth and listen to the local gossip, warmed on chilly days by a pot-bellied stove with a long pipe angling its way to the high ceiling.

Take Kinevan Road rather than 154 on the next leg of the descent. In order to find it, cross 154 and turn left immediately. After about 50 yards a sign says "Not a Through Road"; turn right

53

sharply and down on Kinevan, a narrow, tree-shaded road along San Jose Creek that joins West Camino Cielo before it arrives at 154 (10.3). Head down on 154 for 1.4 miles where a small street sign on the right indicates the turnoff on San Marcos Road (11.7). Take San Marcos down to the starting point at Cathedral Oaks Road (15.3).

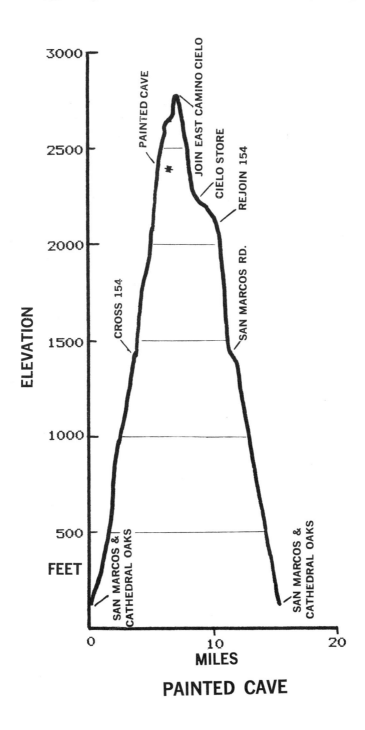

3000

PAINTED CAVE

JOIN EAST CAMINO CIELO

2500

CIELO STORE

REJOIN 154

2000

ELEVATION

SAN MARCOS RD.

CROSS 154

1500

1000

500

SAN MARCOS & CATHEDRAL OAKS

SAN MARCOS & CATHEDRAL OAKS

FEET

0   10   20

MILES

PAINTED CAVE

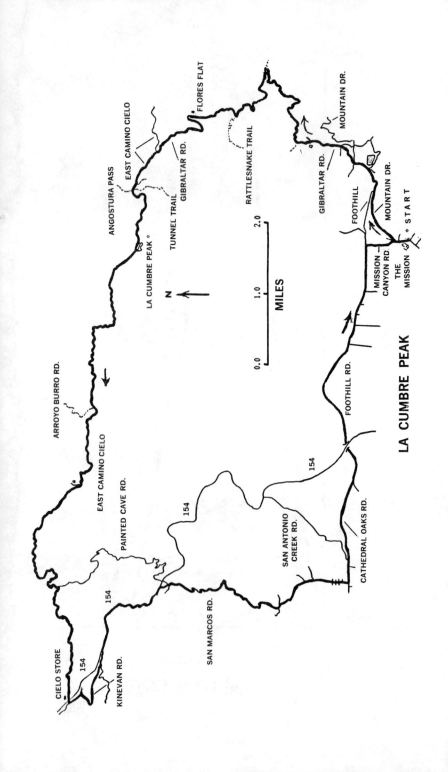

LA CUMBRE PEAK

12

La Cumbre Peak

This spectacular 32-mile loop takes you to the top of the highest nearby mountain (3985 feet) by the way of Gibraltar Road and Camino Cielo—the "Sky Road." It's a toss up as to which direction is best. Taken from east-to-west, the direction I have described here, you climb directly to the peak and then ride up-and-down for 9 mountainous miles to San Marcos Pass, arriving at the Cielo Store and Restaurant for lunch—a timely break before the final downhill run to Cathedral Oaks Road. Unfortunately, however, taken in this direction, you still have 6 miles to go after reaching Cathedral Oaks.

Taken in the other direction, from west-to-east, the break at the Cielo Store happens much earlier, and you are at the peak for lunch time. Because it is spread out over a greater distance, the climb may seem a little easier this way, but the descent is more arduous.

If the mountains are cloud-covered when you start, take clothing. It will be wet and cold. If the mountains are clear and sunny, take two bottles of water. Water is no longer available at the summit. Bring binoculars and maps if you like to identify points on the distant scene. More than most of the routes I have described, this ride gives you a feeling of risk and excitement. The peak looks formidable at the start, but like climbing a mountain—don't worry about the summit. Concentrate on the next step.

Start at the Mission and head toward the mountains. Turn right on Mountain Drive (0.2) and go along the south bank of the valley to the Sheffield Reservoir corner (1.4). Turn left, staying on Mountain Drive. At the intersection with Las Canoas and Gibraltar (1.7), go straight ahead on Gibraltar—the road you will take uphill for the next 6.6 miles. Gibraltar was called "Depression Drive" while it was being built with WPA funds during the 1930's

—in reference to the great economic depression, not to its elevation contour.

At a prominent, eastern-jutting hairpin turn you may see many empty shotgun shell-casings; on weekends the gun-bearers who produce this debris arrive (not on bicycles, however) to add a little more. Broken bottles are found at other places along the edge of the road. Even on this lightly traveled road, you have to look out for the usual cycling hazards. Nonetheless, I find this road more nerve-wracking to take in a car than on a bicycle.

The Rattlesnake Canyon hiking trail joins the road (6.2) before it dips down a bit to Flores Flat (6.9), the site of a ranch. The road then steepens and turns inland along the west wall of Rattlesnake Canyon at the upper end of which it joins East Camino Cielo (8.3).

It levels off then and goes downhill gradually for about 0.5 mile to reach Angostura Pass (9.0) and the upper end of Tunnel Trail. The first panoramic views of the Santa Ynez Valley and the San Rafael Mountains that characterize the next 9 miles of the ride now unfold. A few Joshua trees have begun to appear in the high Chaparral, giving the terrain here a desert-like character.

Leave the pass and climb the final mile to the summit (10.4). Here in addition to terrific views there are: a take off pad for hang-

La Cumbre Peak

gliders, a forest service observation tower (which you may visit when open), a communications station with many dish antennae, picnic tables, and toilets, but no water.

The ride from the summit to San Marcos Pass is up-and-down, but mostly down, until it reaches Arroyo Burro Road (13.6). Then the road ascends for 1.5 miles before starting down again (15.1). After being joined by Painted Cave Road (17.7), it descends through a forest before coming upon the Cielo Store (19.7), just 50 yards before reaching Highway 154 and the San Marcos Pass.

The best way down from the store is by way of Kinevan Road for the first 1.5 miles. Cross 154, turn left immediately, then turn right and down on Kinevan Road. It joins West Camino Cielo before arriving at 154 again (21.1). You have to take busy 154 for about 1.5 miles, but leave it by turning right on San Marcos Road (22.5)—the old road—once called the Santa Ynez Turnpike.

At the bottom turn left on Cathedral Oaks (26.1) and head east for an up-and-down ride on good shoulders until Cathedral Oaks becomes Foothill Road at the 154 underpass (28.0). Foothill is narrow and busy. Leave it after about three miles by turning right on Mission Canyon (31.2) (at a STOP sign), and coast down a gentle slope to the starting point at the Mission (31.9).

Camino Cielo

Miles of fog blown in pennants
across the cold mountain road
a small circle of gray terrain
within the range
of our bound vision.

We stop, stand together
in the hush at the road's edge,
sharing body warmth, and hear
a faint engine hum through the fog
identifying the main road

That will take us back
to a clearer but separate
existence.

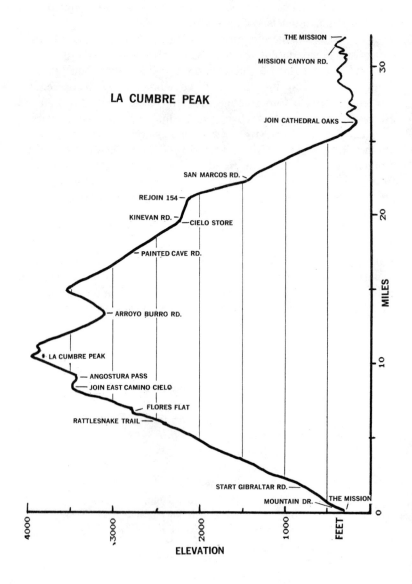

LA CUMBRE PEAK

THE MISSION

MISSION CANYON RD.

JOIN CATHEDRAL OAKS

SAN MARCOS RD.

REJOIN 154

KINEVAN RD.

CIELO STORE

PAINTED CAVE RD.

ARROYO BURRO RD.

★ LA CUMBRE PEAK

ANGOSTURA PASS

JOIN EAST CAMINO CIELO

FLORES FLAT

RATTLESNAKE TRAIL

START GIBRALTAR RD.

MOUNTAIN DR.

THE MISSION

MILES

30

20

10

ELEVATION

4000

3000

2000

1000

FEET

0

SUGGESTED READING

Caltrans: **Pacific Coast Bicentennial Route.** California Department of Transportation, 1976.

Grant, Campbell: **The Rock Paintings of the Chumash.** Univ. of Calif. Press, 1965.

Hudson, Travis: **Guide to Painted Cave.** Santa Barbara, McNally & Loftin, Publishers, 1982.

Kolsbun, Ken & Burgess, Bob: **Discovering Santa Barbara Without a Car.** Santa Barbara, Friends For Bikecology, 1974.

Santa Barbara News Press. Sept. 13, 1964 & Aug. 8, 1965. **(Camanil Crespi story)**

Tompkins, Walker: **Santa Barbara County, California's Wonderful Corner.** Santa Barbara, McNally & Loftin, Publishers, 1962.

Tompkins, Walker: **Santa Barbara Past and Present:** An Illustrated History. Santa Barbara, Tecolote Books, 1975.

LOCAL BICYCLE CLUBS

Goleta Valley Cycling Club: The club for everyone. Call 682-6993. Or write P.O. Box 1547 Goleta, CA 93116.

Santa Barbara Bicycle Club: The local bicycle racing club. P.O. Box 1252 Goleta, CA 93116.

The UCSB Bike Club: For students of the University. Contact Athletics and Leisure Services, University of California, SB, CA 93117.

Energy Cycles: Committed to bicycles as the transportation mode for today. Call 687-1472. Or write P.O. Box 51 Santa Barbara, CA 93102.

For the officers and other current information regarding these clubs, inquire at one of the local bicycle shops.

ABOUT THE AUTHOR

John Lewis is a retired surgeon and computer programmer who lives in Santa Barbara. He has biked in the midwest, in Europe, and up and down the coast, but he prefers Santa Barbara above all.